FRONT COVER: Artistic rendering of Ged Brockie playing a Hofner Senator guitar

Fastlines Jazz Primer

www.guitarandmusicinstitute.com

First published 1992

Copyright 2016 GMI - Guitar & Music Institute

ISBN 978-0-9955088-1-1

All Rights Reserved

No part of this book or mp3s may be reprinted, or reproduced, or utilised in any form by electronic, mechanical or other means, now known or hereafter invented, including photocopying and recording, or in any information retrieval system, without the written permission of the publisher.

Music composed and recorded by Ged Brockie

Gary Fimister - Bass, Dave Stewart - Drums

Recording and mixdown at K.S.M Recording Studios - Edinburgh, Scotland

TABLE OF CONTENTS

FOREWORD..4

AUDIO DOWNLOAD INSTRUCTION...5

QR CODES..6

FASTLINES..12

FASTLINES SOLO..19

BACKING TRACKS..22

PROJECTS..26

PLEASE REVIEW THIS BOOK...30

FOREWORD FROM GED BROCKIE

Thank you for purchasing Fastlines, a work that first saw the light of day back in the early 1990's and through digital technology has now been re designed and re published for a new generation of guitarists.

I have had the joy of performing, teaching and studying the guitar throughout my life. I feel, now more than ever, the pursuit of expression through music and the arts in general can be a transformational experience and a much needed counterweight to the immediacy of the Internet world we now live in.

I created Fastlines so that people could work from a collection of musical ideas that they could use in improvised solo situations. Coming up with lines that make musical sense is one of the great challenges when improvising and that is how the Fastlines concept was born. As well as this, I wanted to provide an understanding of how each line functioned. Through this understanding, lines could be altered and changed to fit various harmonic scenarios. The short solo that is included in this book offers the student insight into ways in which different lines can be joined together to create a meaningful improvisation. Backing tracks give context for each of the memorised lines to be realised and heard against and finally, the projects allow for long term development of the lines presented here.

I hope you enjoy using this work and that you will consider the other books in the series which were developed over a two year period. I am confident that they will bring you a deeper understanding of the jazz genre and help you meet your improvisational goals.

Ged Brockie

Ged Brockie has performed in almost every conceivable musical scenario over a thirty year period. His own band recordings comprise his own compositions, arrangements and performance with some of Scotland's finest musicians (The Mirror's Image - Circular Records 2009, The Last View From Mary's Place - Circular Records 2004). He was one of the main writers in the Scottish Guitar Quartet (SGQ) recording three albums (Near The Circle 2001, Fait Accompli 2003, Landmarks 2005) touring across Europe to critical acclaim. The DVD "Five Innovations For Guitar & Orchestra - Circular Records 2011" featured Ged with a twenty one piece orchestra. He has also worked with the RSNO, OSO, Carl Davis, Hummie Mann, West End shows on tour, TV & radio, music industry events, all levels of music education from high school to university and has a wide range of compositions used in film, TV and media.

Ged is the lead instructor and driving force behind GMI and guides the programs of learning within it.

www.gedbrockie.com

HAVE YOU DOWNLOADED YOUR AUDIO FILES YET?

1. Book owners should access mp3 files for this book at the following URL…This is NOT a necessary step if you just wish to use the QR codes provided in this book.

   http://www.guitarandmusicinstitute/audiojazzprimerfl/

2. For security purposes and in an effort to try and keep piracy to a bearable level you will be asked three questions which relate to words found on pages within this book. You will also be asked for your name and email.

3. A compressed file containing all the mp3 files will be downloadable from a link contained within an email that will be sent to the email address you have stipulated on correct completion of the questions.

4. Make sure to check your spam folder regarding this email just incase nothing turn up within five to ten minutes.

5. Thank you for purchasing this book and supporting further publications from GMI, we really do appreciate it.

FASTLINES
QR CODES & LINES

QR CODES

QR CODES FOR VIDEO ON YOUR PHONE OR TABLET!

FASTLINES intro and tuning up notes

The above image is a QR code. These have been provided so you don't need to turn on a computer and quickly hear the relevant audio on your mobile phone or tablet whilst at your music stand.

1. Download a QR code reader from Google Play or the Mac store. There are many free programs.

2. Once downloaded, open up the app and point at the QR code. The relevant mp3 will open for you to play.

3. We tried to embed QR codes beside each musical example, however, there were issues regarding the small size of the QR code as well as spacing and the relevant mp3 file being activated. These pages provide a list for you to refer to and use when studying a specific line, the solo or Backtracks.

QR code for Fastline 1 Jazz Primer

QR code for Fastline 2 Jazz Primer

QR code for Fastline 3 Jazz Primer

QR code for Fastline 4 Jazz Primer

QR CODES Cont...

QR code for Fastline 5 Jazz Primer

QR code for Fastline 6 Jazz Primer

QR code for Fastline 7 Jazz Primer

QR code for Fastline 8 Jazz Primer

QR code for Fastline 9 Jazz Primer

QR code for Fastline 10 Jazz Primer

QR code for Fastline 11 Jazz Primer

QR CODES Cont...

QR code for Fastline 12 Jazz Primer

QR code for Fastline 13 Jazz Primer

QR code for Fastline 14 Jazz Primer

QR code for Fastline 15 Jazz Primer

QR code for Fastline 16 Jazz Primer

QR code for Fastline 17 Jazz Primer

QR code for Fastline 18 Jazz Primer

QR CODES Cont...

QR code for Fastline 19 Jazz Primer

QR code for Fastline 20 Jazz Primer

QR code for Fastline Jazz Primer solo

QR code for Jazz Primer Backtrack 1

QR code for Jazz Primer Backtrack 2

QR code for Jazz Primer Backtrack 3

FASTLINES Jazz Primer by Ged Brockie

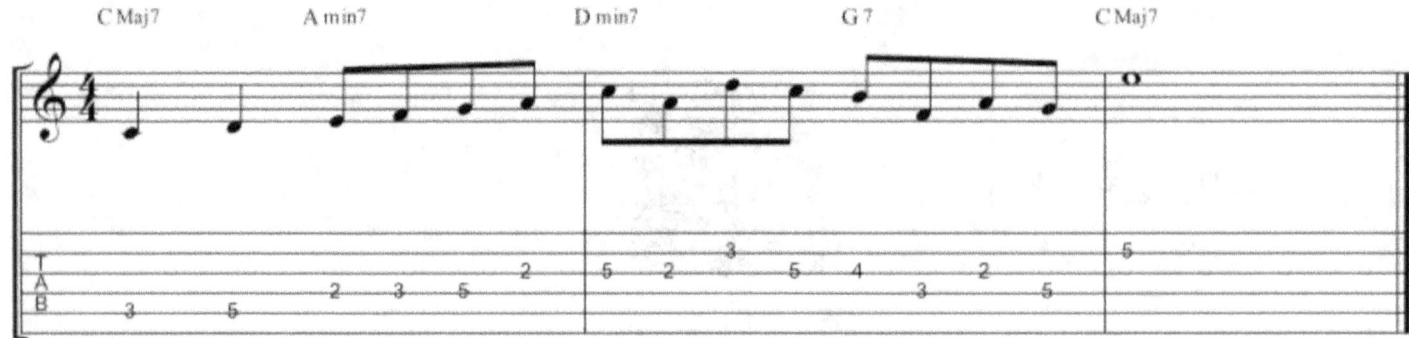

FASTLINE One Tempo: 120
Scale used: C major.
Tech./harmonic aspects: Step wise movement of C major scale. Outlining of chords in second bar.
Comments:
1. An easy idea to start with. Concentrate on playing with a full rounded sound (no glitches) and with a swing feel. Use alternate picking strokes throughout.

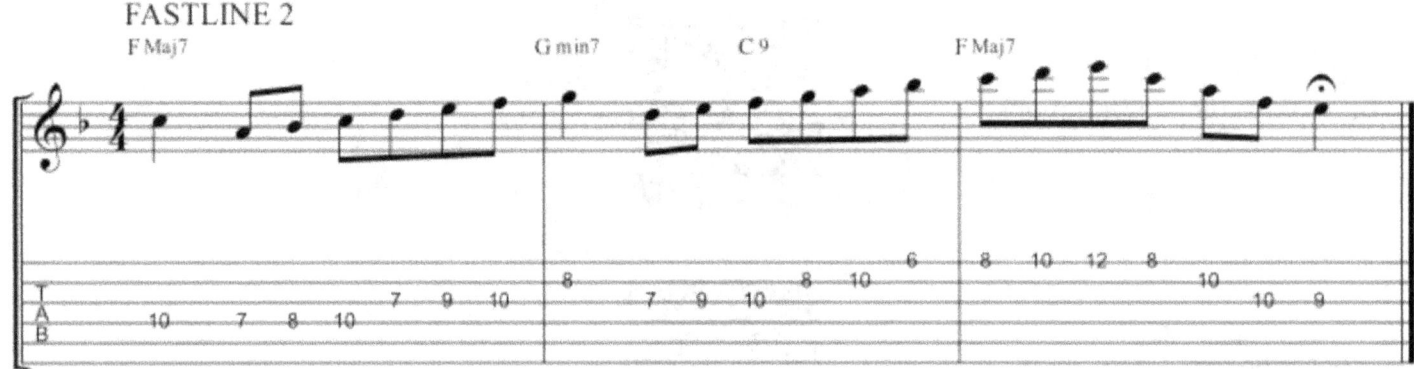

FASTLINE Two Tempo: 116
Scale used: F major.
Tech./harmonic aspects: Scalar runs, F major seven arpeggio, repeated rhythmic pattern, position shifting.
Comments:
1. This whole Fastline evolved from the first bar idea. To continue the scalar pattern a position/finger change is needed in the middle of bar two.
2. The line ends with a descending F major seven arpeggio which is very much a Jazz cliche.

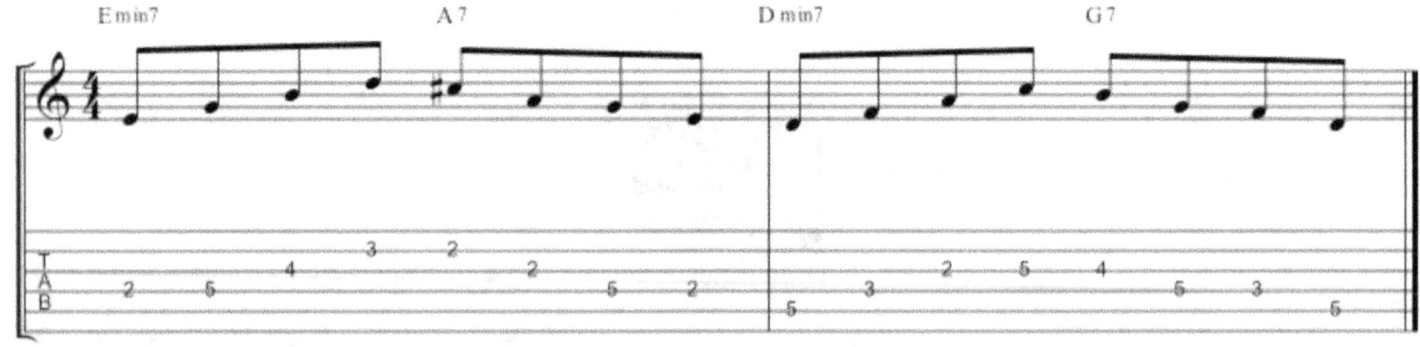

FASTLINE Three Tempo: 126
Scales used: D major/C major.
Tech./harmonic aspects: Use of arpeggios to outline each of the chords notated.
Comments:
1. Very popular substitution for two bars of C major. Only the fundamental tones (no extended notes) have been used.

FASTLINE 4

FASTLINE Four Tempo: 120
Scale used: G major.
Tech./harmonic aspects: Various melodic con- tours used throughout the line. D7 arpeggio.
Comments:
1. The fifth chord in the key of G major (D7 arpeggio) has been substituted over the G major chord at the beginning of this Fastline.

FASTLINE 5

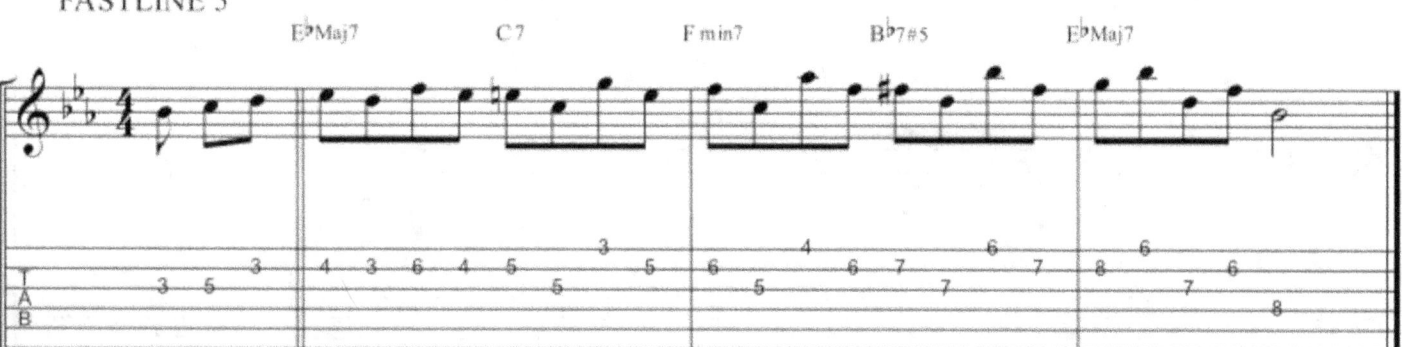

FASTLINE Five Tempo: 112
Scale used: E flat major.
Tech./harmonic aspects: Inner line movement, outlining of chords, string skipping.
Comments:
1. This Fastline would work well over an ending to create a turnaround. You may find that the lower notes prove quite difficult to execute in tempo.

FASTLINE 6

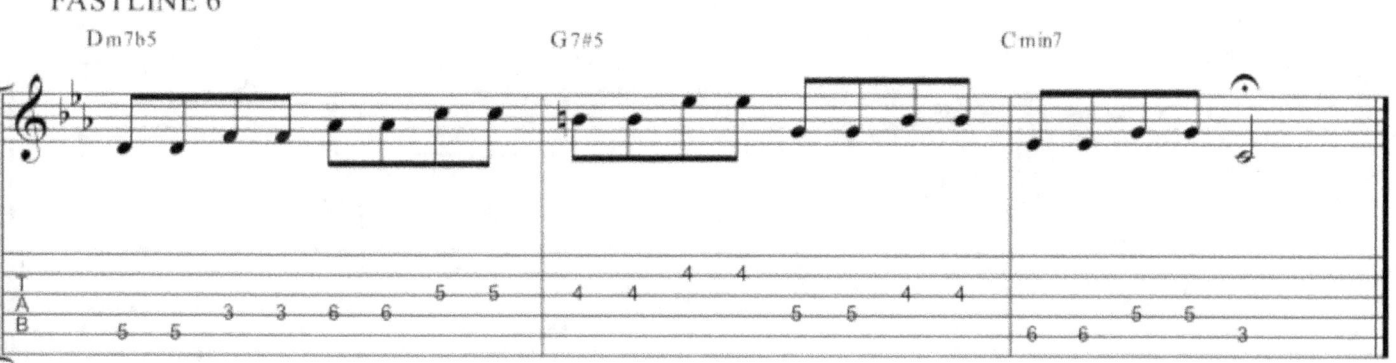

FASTLINE Six Tempo: 132
Scale used: C harmonic minor.
Tech./harmonic aspects: Repeated notes, use of arpeggios for each chord, rolling technique needed from the left hand fingers.
Comments:
1. The repeating of each note in Fastline six would make good exercise material.

FASTLINE 7

FASTLINE Seven Tempo: 108
Scale used: F major (Locrian mode), A whole-tone, D melodic minor.
Tech./harmonic aspects: Scalar passages, arpeggios, stretch fingerings.
Comments:
1. The line consists of several scalar substitutions that you should memorise. F major scale being played over E minor seven flat five (half-step up) and "A" whole-tone over A7 to produce altered tones.

FASTLINE 8

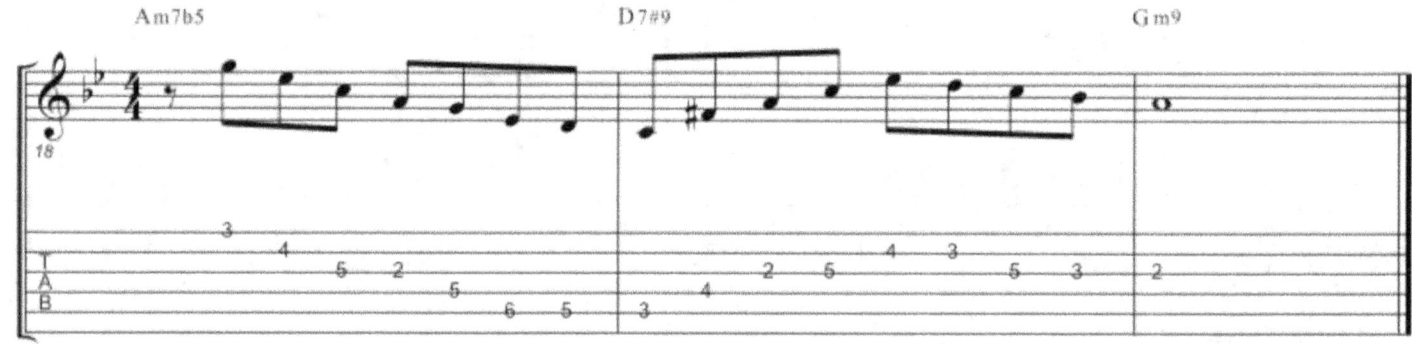

FASTLINE Eight Tempo: 116
Scale used: G minor harmonic.
Tech./harmonic aspects: Arpeggios, stretch fingering.
Comments:
1. The idea played over D7 sharp nine consists of an F sharp diminished arpeggio.

FASTLINE 9

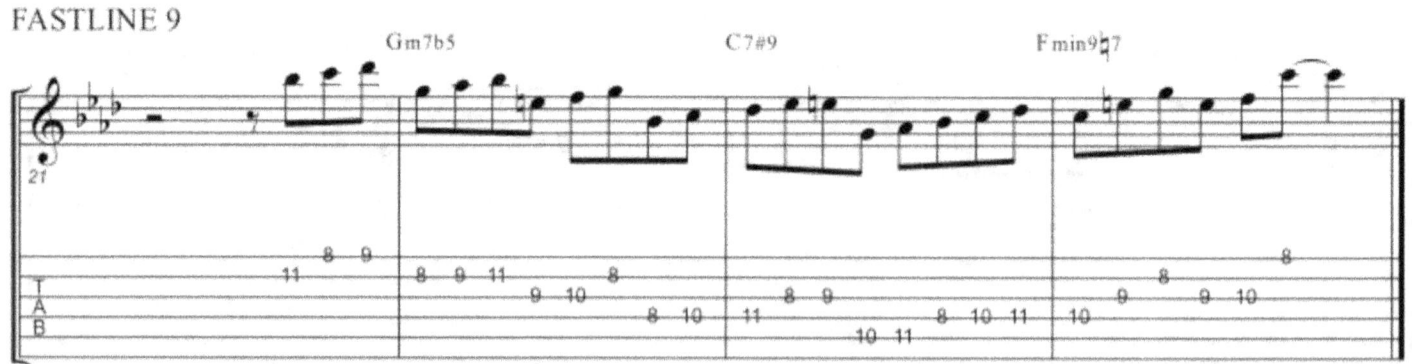

FASTLINE Nine Tempo: 112
Scales used: F harmonic minor.
Tech./harmonic aspects: Melodic contours used throughout this Fastline, line is rhythmically offset from the start.
Comments:
1. If you are not used to playing further up the guitar neck, then Fastline nine should give you a good work-out. The line could easily be moved along to start on beat one with the note B flat.

FASTLINE 10

FASTLINE Ten   Tempo: 132

Scale used: A minor harmonic.

Tech./harmonic aspects: Breaking up the arpeggio, stretch fingerings, melodic contours.

Comments:

1. The problem to address here is the stretch fingering needed to shift from the first to the second bar. If you are not used to playing arpeggios, then try playing this idea up one octave as well.

FASTLINE 11

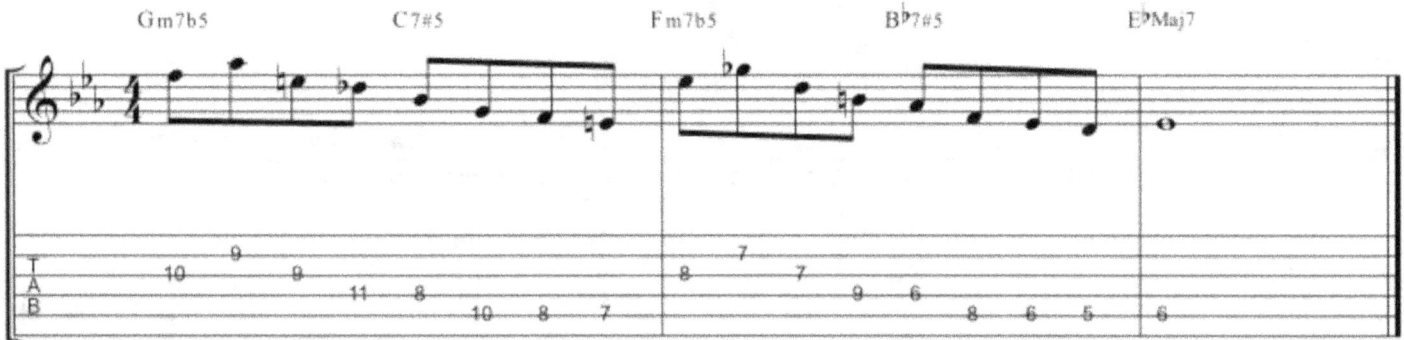

FASTLINE Eleven   Tempo: 116

Scales used: F and E flat harmonic minors.

Tech./harmonic aspects: Diminished chords, repeated patterns transposed down one tone.

Comments:

1. There are numerous examples within standard Jazz progressions where the major chord is approached by a minor II-V progression. This Fastline includes a repeated figure over two bars.

2. The substitution of a diminished arpeggio over a dominant seventh chord is found in bars one and two. This idea is used further in the second Fastline tutor in this series.

FASTLINE 12

FASTLINE Twelve   Tempo: 138

Scale used: D major.

Tech./harmonic aspects: Scalar runs, chromatic approach notes, intervals.

Comments:

1. This idea is relatively easy to learn and sounds very effective when played at faster tempos. The chromatic approach tones (E flat, B flat, F natural) help to fill the line out and generate a Blues feel. Remember to sustain the last two notes of the line into each other.

FASTLINE 13

FASTLINE Thirteen   Tempo: 152

Scale used: C major.

Tech./harmonic aspects: Melodic contours, string skipping.

Comments:

1. Rhythmically, Fastline thirteen is very similar to Fastline nine. Thirteen shows how a rhythmic idea can precede the melodic content.
2. Bar two contains a two string skip.

FASTLINE 14

FASTLINE Fourteen   Tempo: 132

Scale used: G major.

Tech./harmonic aspects: Rhythmic repetition of scalar passages, repeated notes, chromatic approach tones.

Comments:

1. This line should not pose too many problems. Try to ensure that you don't rush any one phrase.

FASTLINE 15

FASTLINE Fifteen   Tempo: 144

Scale used: B flat major.

Tech./harmonic aspects: Scalar runs, major seventh arpeggio.

Comments:

1. The B flat major scale is used to outline the C minor seven and F dominant seven chords as well as the tonic chord B flat major.

FASTLINE 16

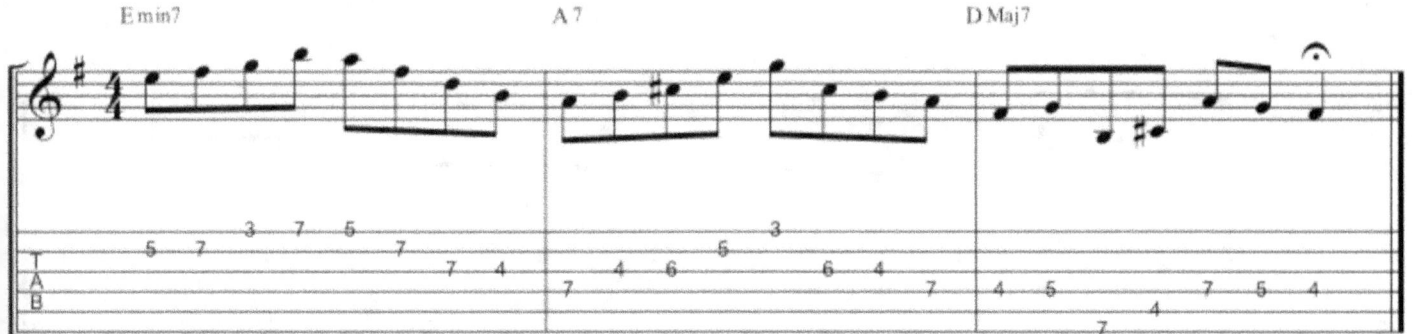

FASTLINE Sixteen Tempo: 120
Scale used: D major.
Tech./harmonic aspects: Scalar runs, B minor seven arpeggio substituting over Em7, string skipping, large interval leaps, rolling left hand finger technique.
Comments:
1. After the previous three Fastlines, number sixteen should prove quite a different proposition. Each bar contains awkward sections as in the string skips in bar two (beat three) and in bar three (beat three). Practise these sections in isolation if they prove difficult.

FASTLINE 17

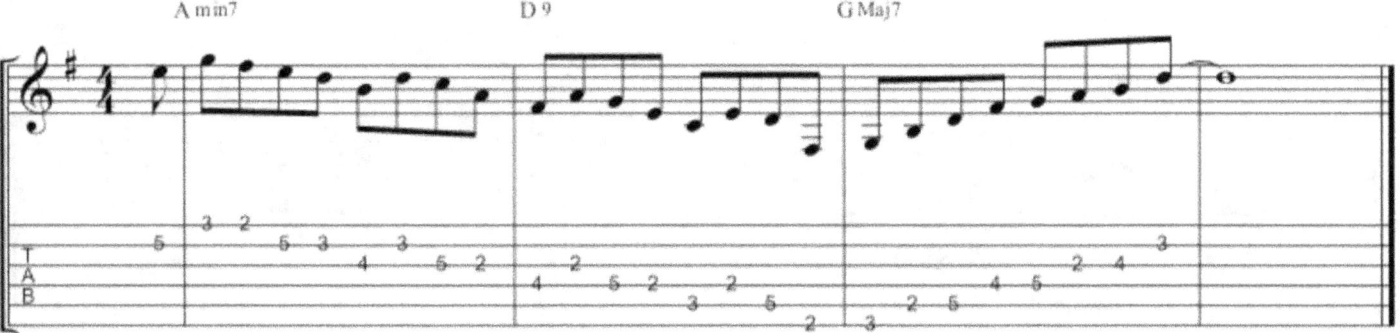

FASTLINE Seventeen Tempo: 144
Scale used: G major.
Tech./harmonic aspects: Scalar and melodic contour passages, G major seven arpeggio.
Comments:
1. This line is very similar in content to the previous Fastline but in the new key of G major. Notice how, for the most part, fundamental tones are stressed on the strong part of the beat. Keep this in mind when analysing solos or making up your own ideas.

FASTLINE 18

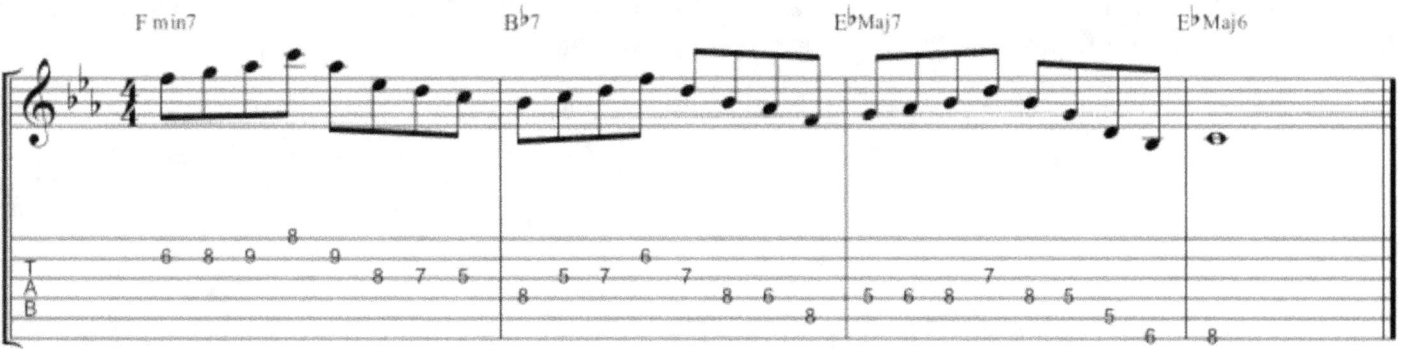

FASTLINE Eighteen Tempo: 138
Scale used: E flat major.
Tech./harmonic aspects: Use of motifs, E flat major seventh arpeggio, B flat dominant seven arpeggio.
Comments:
1. The motif idea is stated in the first two beats of bar one and is used throughout the line. This idea was used to great effect by John Coltrane over the changes to his composition Giant Steps. Motif development is a huge subject and one that you should consider studying in depth.

FASTLINE 19

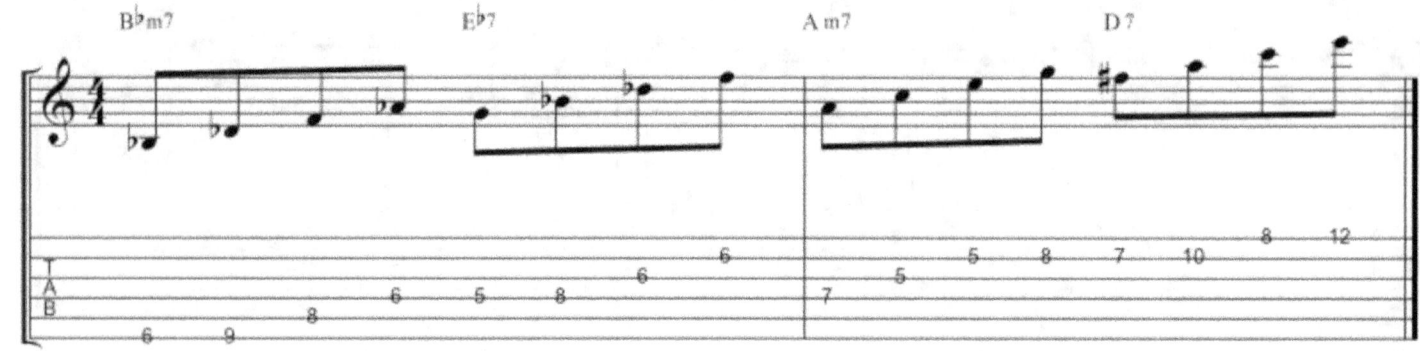

FASTLINE Nineteen Tempo: 152

Scales used: A flat/G major.

Tech./harmonic aspects: B flat minor seven, E flat dominant seven, A minor seven and D dominant seven, stretch fingers, positional changes.

Comments:

1. This is the first of two Fastlines which address the movement of chords chromatically. The content of the second is exactly the same as the first, but one octave higher. The positional changes should pose no real challenge, although finger stretches for the left hand may cause some discomfort.

FASTLINE 20

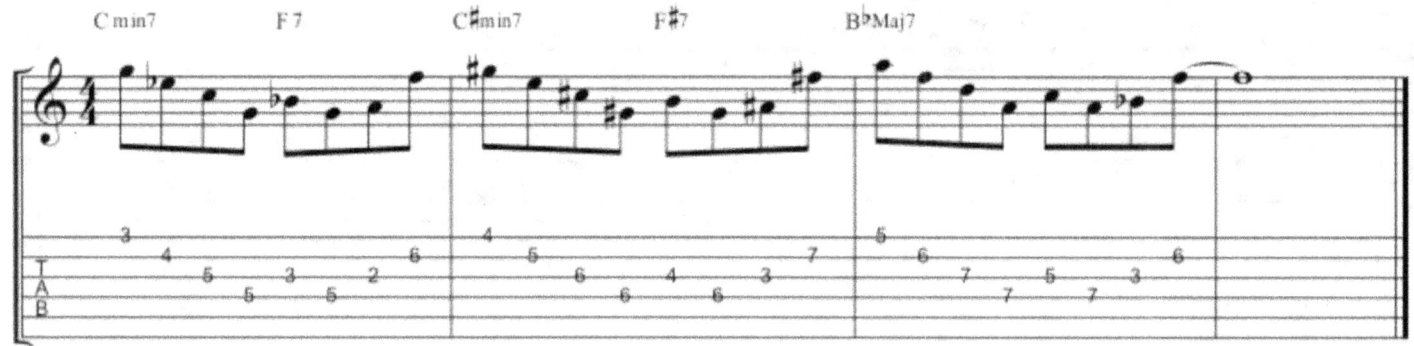

FASTLINE Twenty Tempo: 160

Scales used: B flat/B natural major.

Tech./harmonic aspects: Stretch fingering, movable physical shape used, all the respective arpeggios of the chords notated.

Comments:

1. Interesting harmonic variation for use over the familiar II-V-I progression. Once you have mastered bar one, you then play the entire line. Try and visualise the shapes being used to aid memorisation.

FASTLINES SOLO

FASTLINE Solo

The Fastline solo contains most, if not all, of the techniques outlined in the line by line section. Several Fastlines have been lifted directly out of the Fastline lick section and placed in the solo, and new ideas have also been added. For more details of the Fastline solo, and how to get the best out of it, turn to the projects section found later in this booklet.

Bars 1-4: II-V-I in the key of A minor. Fastline ten used in bars two-four.
Bars 5-8: II-V-I-IV in the key of C major. Idea is based upon Fastline thirteen.
Bars 9-10: Again, a II-V idea in A minor. This part of the solo uses Fastline number eight. The Fastline used had to change key from G to A minor by raising the whole line up a tone.
Bars 11-12: The last two bars of A minor uses wide interval jumps. The solo ends with A and B notes being played together to create a minor 2nd interval.

Note: To play along with the backing chords to the solo, simply pan speakers left or right. Tempo 112 bpm

BACKING TRACKS

FASTLINE PROJECTS

FASTLINES JAZZ PRIMER PROJECTS

Arpeggio playing

If you are new to the art of playing Jazz guitar then learning to play over chord progressions (called changes) is a priority. Fastline number three shows arpeggios played over four chords using only the fundamental tones of each chord (root, third, fifth, seventh). The starting note for each new chord begins with a different fundamental tone - the root for Em7, the fifth for A7, the flattened third for Dm7 and the flattened seventh for G7. Note how well the different arpeggios fit together when linking up these tones.

By using this Fastline as your example, work out more arpeggio shapes then attempt to join them together smoothly. The existing progressions given in this Fastline booklet will give you plenty of material to work from.

Inner-lines

The use of inner lines in your musical phrases will give your solos greater musical depth. Fastline five has an ascending chromatic line played on beats one and three of each bar (E flat, E natural, F natural, F sharp, G natural). The rest of the notes have been moulded around this idea which is the backbone of the line.

Inner lines need not be chromatic or ascending to work well, but some sort of repetition and movement either up or down works best. Many Jazz guitarists have studied the music of Johann Sebastian Bach as his music contains many examples of this type of melodic development. If you would like to study this subject further then Bach s Partitas are a good place to start.

Several of the Fastlines in this booklet are made up from arpeggios and would provide a good platform from which to introduce inner-line movement.

Altered chords

You will have noticed that many dominant seventh chords have been notated with sharpened and flattened fifth and ninth tones. In terms of soloing, it is preferable to include the altered notes in order to express each chord correctly and create tension or dissonance over the cadence points of a chord progression.

The whole-tone scale provides us with most of these altered tones. In Fastline seven, bar two, the A whole-tone scale is played in its entirety. In preparation for the Intermediate tutor, you should practise this scale daily. Play from the root note, A, up one octave to A on the first string using different fingers of the left hand to start with. Although this scale will sound odd at first, you will find that after several weeks this sound will become familiar.

Spicing it up

You need not take a constant linear approach when playing arpeggio patterns, i.e., root, third, fifth and seventh. Fastline ten opens with good examples in bar one and two of how to stimulate interest by breaking up the usual arpeggio shapes. For example, here are some ideas to introduce to your practise schedule with regards to arpeggios.

Root, fifth, third, seventh - fifth, seventh, root, third and third, fifth, seventh, root. There are obviously many more combinations which can be generated and you will find that, with constant practise, they will begin to show themselves in your improvisations.

Scalar approach

Fastline fifteen provides a simple but effective scalar line over a II-V-I progression.

Jazz guitar soloing, at its simplest, is the gelling together of arpeggios and scales. To do this, a firm understanding in both theoretical and practical terms is needed. The home or tonic scale in this example is B flat major. Being able to play major scales over the entire fretboard is not only desirable but necessary.

Try playing Fastline fifteen over several octaves. Find as many different fingerings and positions on the fretboard as possible. By using musical phrases as in Fastline fifteen, scale memorisation will become more interesting and help develop your musical ear.

Chromatic movement

Trying to play through chord progressions that move chromatically up or down the guitar fretboard presents great difficulty for beginners. This is because the key centres of the music continually change. Fastlines nineteen and twenty are included to help you start working in this area. Listen to Fastline nineteen and hear how well it works. The second bar is an exact copy of the first bar but played up one octave and down a semi-tone (A flat major moving to G major). Write out the other eleven major key centre II-V-I progressions then join any two that are separated by one semi-tone either above or below. Start playing suitable Fastline ideas over both key centres in each case.

Altering the aspect of the chords used to major, minor or dominant sevenths will increase the scope of this project.

Backward motion

Record yourself playing the chords for each Fastline given in the booklet. Take each Fastline in turn and play each bar within it from it's right hand side. The resulting sounds that you end up with should provide you with at least ten to fifteen more Fastline ideas.

This approach to learning new material may seem a little unartistic, but it's through the changing and mixing up of existing ideas that new sounds will present themselves.

Picking techniques

If you are new to playing plectrum guitar then building a solid platform from which to work from is essential. Right hand picking technique is an area that causes many guitarists years of trouble. No single technique can be viewed as the definitive one, but keep in mind that whatever your chosen method is, it must be used in a consistent manner.

All the Fastlines in this booklet have been composed in such a way that constant up and down strokes (alternate picking) can be used throughout. In later tutors, the introduction of hammer-ons and pull-offs makes a less rigid approach necessary and modifications can be applied.

For now, concentrate on alternate picking for each Fastline. Take some of the harder examples and try sweep, or three notes per string ideas on them with an eye to your future development.

Callisthenics

Proper warm-up exercises are as essential to the guitarist as they are to the sportsman. The name given to these warm-up exercises is Callisthenics. Callisthenics are short, easy to memorise ideas that help to build and keep in shape co-ordination and stamina for both left and right hands.

There may have been several Fastlines in this tutor that you had difficulty with passages that were hard to execute cleanly or caused left hand picking problems. These are just the kind of ideas that you can isolate and use as a daily warm-up routine.

The areas that you should be looking to exercise daily in are: right and left hand co-ordination with regards to picking, left hand stretch exercises and speed picking.

A daily warm-up session need not be any longer than ten minutes but its effect on your playing will last much longer.

Fastline solo

Each Fastline tutor in the jazz series comes with a short solo to let the student hear just how effective Fastline ideas sound when joined together in a tasteful way. The aim of this project is the same as in each of the other solo projects in the jazz guitar tutors, namely, to encourage you to link together, by way of transposition, the Fastlines you have learned.

Jazz musicians use a set of popular songs, both old and new, to improvise over. These tunes are usually referred to as "standards". If you are serious about playing jazz guitar, then you should acquiring a volume named "The Fake Book". The Fake Book is packed with standard songs that contain both easy and challenging chord progressions and great melodies.

If you already own a Fake Book, then now is the time to start linking up Fastlines over your favourite titles. By doing this many times and by memorising the results, you will build up a vocabulary of phrases from which to use when in improvising situations.

PLEASE REVIEW AND STAR RATE THIS BOOK

If you have found this book helpful in your guitar playing development, please take the time to give a review and give the book a star rating. We value your contribution and it helps us when creating more resources for guitarists around the world.

Thanks for your time. Please visit us at the following URL address:

http://www.guitarandmusicinstitute.com